INTERMEDIATE/ADVANCED PIANO

M000159857

Dan Coates
POPULAR PIANO SOLOS

THE
PROFESSIONAL *Touch*

(800) 876-9777
10075 SW Beav-Hills Hwy (503) 641-5691
733 SW 10th (503) 228-6659
12334 SE Division (503) 760-6881

Project Manager: Zobeida Pérez
Art Layout: Ken Rehm

DAN COATES® is a registered trademark of Warner Bros. Publications

Dan Coates

As a student at the University of Miami, Dan Coates paid his tuition by playing the piano at south Florida nightclubs and restaurants. One evening in 1975, after Dan had worked his unique brand of magic on the ivories, a stranger from the music field walked up and told him that he should put his inspired piano arrangements down on paper so they could be published.

Dan took the stranger's advice—and the world of music has become much richer as a result. Since that chance encounter long ago, Dan has gone on to achieve international acclaim for his brilliant piano arrangements. His *Big Note, Easy Piano* and *Professional Touch* arrangements have inspired countless piano students and established themselves as classics against which all other works must be measured.

Enjoying an exclusive association with Warner Bros. Publications since 1982, Dan has demonstrated a unique gift for writing arrangements intended for students of every level, from beginner to advanced. Dan never fails to bring a fresh and original approach to his work. Pushing his own creative boundaries with each new manuscript, he writes material that is musically exciting and educationally sound.

From the very beginning of his musical life, Dan has always been eager to seek new challenges. As a five-year-old in Syracuse, New York, he used to sneak into the home of his neighbors to play their piano. Blessed with an amazing ear for music, Dan was able to imitate the melodies of songs he had heard on the radio. Finally, his neighbors convinced his parents to buy Dan his own piano. At that point, there was no stopping his musical development. Dan won a prestigious New York State competition for music composers at the age of 15. Then, after graduating from high school, he toured the world as an arranger and pianist with the group Up With People.

Later, Dan studied piano at the University of Miami with the legendary Ivan Davis, developing his natural abilities to stylize music on the keyboard. Continuing to perform professionally during and after his college years, Dan has played the piano on national television and at the 1984 Summer Olympics in Los Angeles. He has also accompanied recording artists as diverse as Dusty Springfield and Charlotte Rae.

During his long and prolific association with Warner Bros. Publications, Dan has written many award-winning books. He conducts piano workshops worldwide, demonstrating his famous arrangements with a special spark that never fails to inspire students and teachers alike.

BIO01 2/23/04

CONTENTS

AMAZED

Words and Music by
MARV GREEN, AIMEE MAYO
and CHRIS LINDSEY
Arranged by DAN COATES

Slowly (♩ = 76)

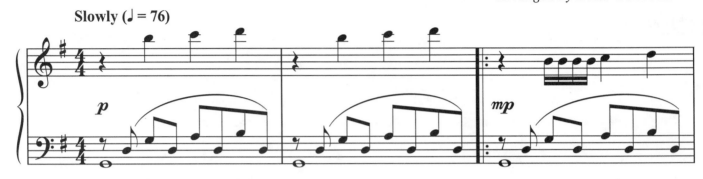

(with pedal)

AND ALL THAT JAZZ

Words by FRED EBB

Music by JOHN KANDER
Arranged by DAN COATES

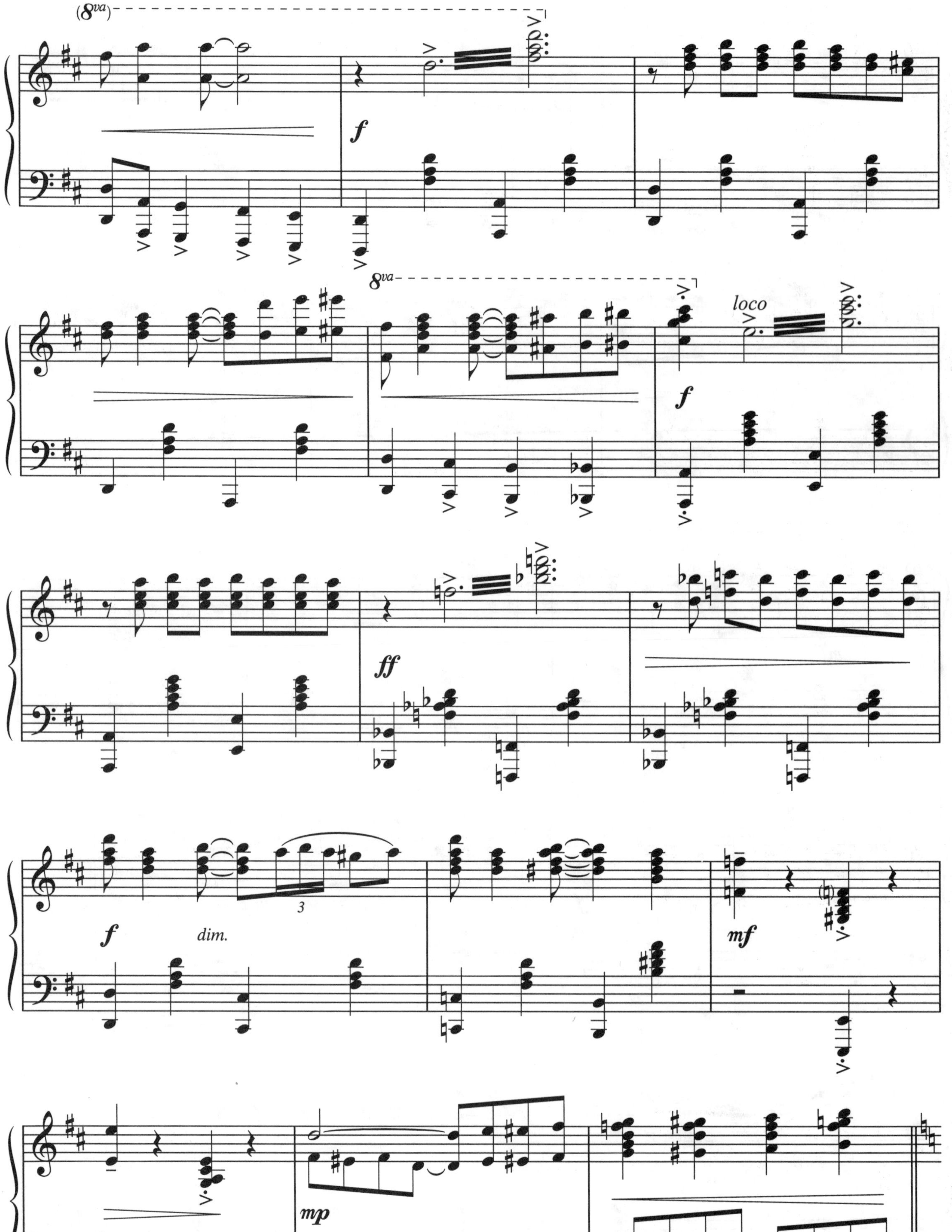
(8va)
f
8va
loco
f
ff
f
dim.
3
mf
mp

From THE POLAR EXPRESS

BELIEVE

Words and Music by
GLEN BALLARD and ALAN SILVESTRI
Arranged by DAN COATES

DANCE WITH MY FATHER

Words and Music by
LUTHER VANDROSS
and RICHARD MARX
Arranged by DAN COATES

Dance With My Father - 5 - 3
AFM0504

BRIDGE OVER TROUBLED WATER

Words and Music by
PAUL SIMON
Arranged by DAN COATES

Slowly, like a spiritual ♩ = 72

Bridge Over Troubled Water - 6 - 1
AFM0504

Bridge Over Troubled Water - 6 - 2
AFM0504

DON'T CRY OUT LOUD

Words and Music by
PETER ALLEN and CAROLE BAYER SAGER
Arranged by DAN COATES

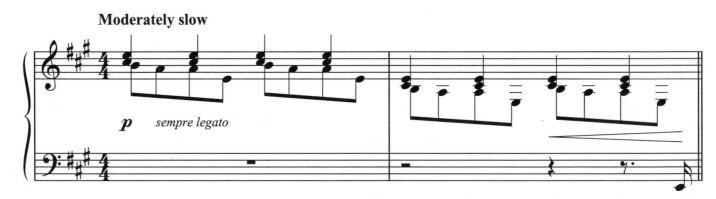

Don't Cry Out Loud - 4 - 1
AFM0504

Don't Cry Out Loud - 4 - 2
AFM0504

THE NOTEBOOK
(Main Title)

Written by
AARON ZIGMAN
Arranged by DAN COATES

The Notebook - 3 - 1
AFM0504

THIS I PROMISE YOU

Words and Music by
RICHARD MARX
Arranged by DAN COATES

Slowly (♩ = 84)

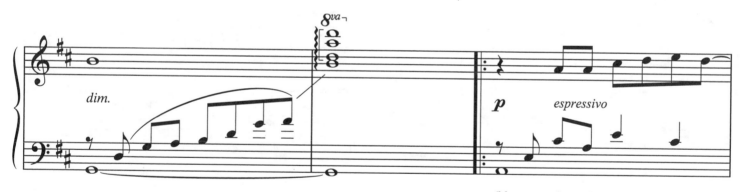

This I Promise You - 5 - 1
AFM0504

This I Promise You - 5 - 3
AFM0504

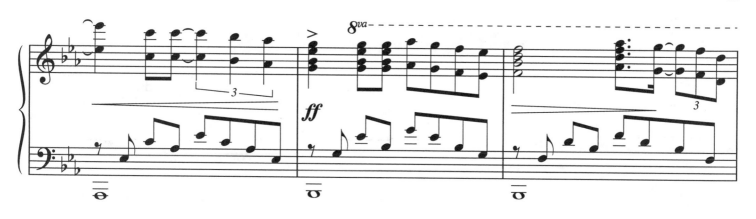

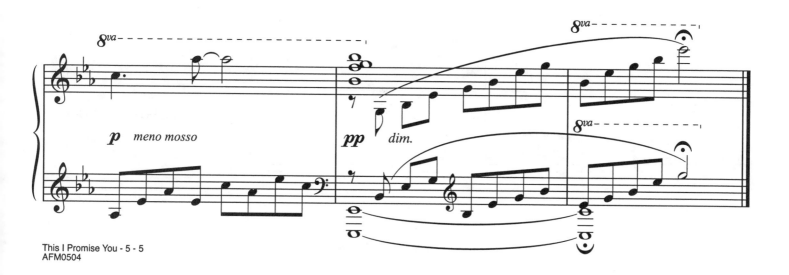

From Touchstone Pictures' PEARL HARBOR

THERE YOU'LL BE

Words and Music by
DIANE WARREN
Arranged by DAN COATES

43

There You'll Be - 4 - 2
AFM0504

YOU NEEDED ME

Words and Music by
RANDY GOODRUM
Arranged by DAN COATES

Slowly, with expression

(l.h. simile throughout)

You Needed Me - 4 - 2
AFM0504

TO WHERE YOU ARE

Words and Music by
RICHARD MARX and
LINDA THOMPSON
Arranged by DAN COATES

Slowly, with expression (♩ = 69)

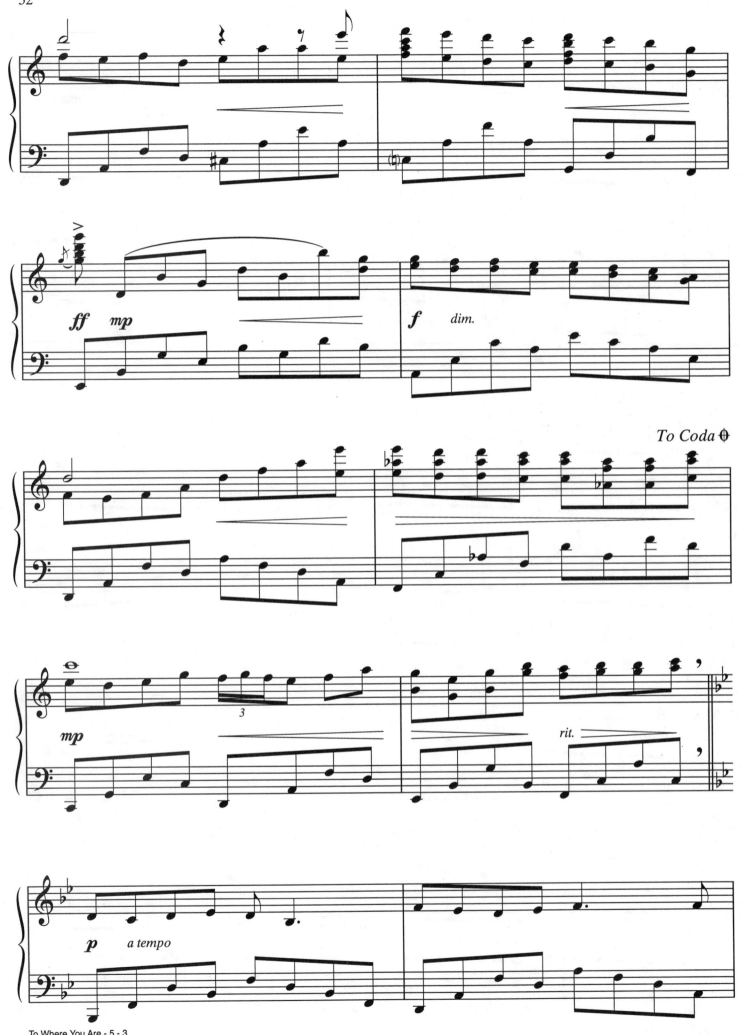

D.S. ℅ al Coda

⊕ Coda

YOU RAISE ME UP

Words and Music by
ROLF LOVLAND
and BRENDAN GRAHAM
Arranged by DAN COATES

56

New Series by Dan Coates!

Teacher's Choice! Dan Coates Pop Keyboard Library

Designed to work with any piano method, this series offers an outstanding source of pedagogically sound supplementary material that is fun and exciting and will appeal to today's piano student. Specifically graded and with fingerings at each level, these books will expand any student's course of study, giving them incentive to practice and play more.

- **The early levels (Books 1 and 2) have teacher accompaniment parts, and the titles have been carefully selected to appeal to the younger student (children's songs, patriotic music, folk songs, cartoon themes).**

- **Book 3 offers more pop titles, including music from *Harry Potter, Star Wars*, and even some Disney favorites.**

- **Books 4 and 5 (intermediate and advanced) cater to teen and adult players with great pop hits and standards, including the best movie themes and chart-topping pop ballads.**

BOOK 1, Early Elementary
Titles are: America, the Beautiful • Little Sir Echo • The Merry-Go-Round Broke Down • On Top of Old Smokey • Take Me Out to the Ball Game • This Land Is Your Land • This Old Man • Twinkle, Twinkle, Little Star • When the Saints Go Marching In • The Yankee Doodle Boy.
(AFM0205)

BOOK 2, Mid-Elementary
Titles are: Jeopardy Theme • Lullaby and Goodnight • The Muffin Man • Ode to Joy (Theme from Beethoven's *Ninth Symphony*) • Over the Rainbow (from *The Wizard of Oz*) • She'll Be Coming 'Round the Mountain • The Song That Doesn't End • This Is It! (Theme from "The Bugs Bunny Show") • Today • You Are My Sunshine.
(AFM0206)

BOOK 3, Late Elementary
Titles are: Daisy, Daisy • (Meet) The Flintstones • Happy Wanderer • Harry's Wondrous World (from *Harry Potter and the Sorcerer's Stone*) • I Believe I Can Fly • I've Been Working on the Railroad • Somewhere Out There (from *An American Tail*) • Star Wars (Main Title) • Theme from *Ice Castles* (Through the Eyes of Love) • Theme from *Inspector Gadget* • Tomorrow • A Whole New World.
(AFM0207)

BOOK 4, Early Intermediate to Intermediate
Titles are: Candle in the Wind • Circle of Life • Hedwig's Theme (from *Harry Potter and the Sorcerer's Stone*) • I Hope You Dance • In Dreams (from *The Lord of the Rings*) • The James Bond Theme • The Pink Panther • Send in the Clowns • Somewhere My Love (from *Dr. Zhivago*) • Theme from *E.T. (The Extra-Terrestrial)* • To Love You More • Your Song.
(AFM0208)

BOOK 5, Late Intermediate to Advanced
Titles are: All By Myself • Amazed • Don't Cry for Me, Argentina (from *Evita*) • From This Moment On • The Prayer • Somewhere in Time • Somewhere Out There • Theme from *Schindler's List* • Time to Say Goodbye • Valentine.
(AFM0209)

AD1099 1/03